How an Orb is Created or Caused
By Lee Steer
www.project-reveal.com

Http://www.facebook.com/projectreveal
http://www.youtube.com/projectghosts

Certified Android App Developer
https://play.google.com/store/apps/developer?id=project+reveal

Thank you for taking interest in our book on orbs.

Orbs is thought to be the first sign of a spirit manifestation, people believe that Ghosts, spirits can show them self's in little balls of lights, Known as Orbs..

Throughout the book we will discuss all different types of orbs, what causes orbs; we have compiled a lot of data and pictures to help you understand your journey into Orbs

How an Orb is Created

This book will show you a number of ways orbs are made or caused

There are a number of natural causes for orbs in photography and videography which include:

Dry partical matter such as dust, pollen, insects, etc.

Droplets of liquid, moisture

Foreign material on the camera lens

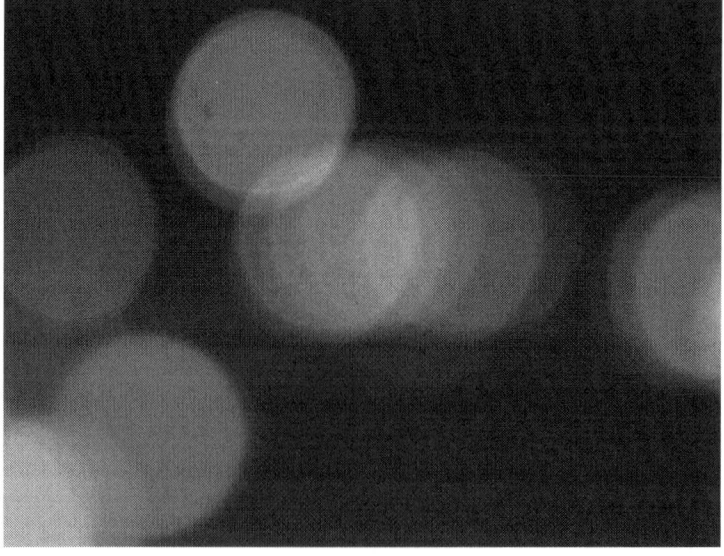

Foreign material within the camera lens

THE ALFRED PLAQUE

This plaque was erected in 1986 to mark the eleven hundredth anniversary of King Alfred's resettlement of the Roman city of London in 886, after the abandonment of the Saxon town which had existed for some three centuries in the Strand area to the west of the City. At this place a harbour and market were established by 899 to restore trade after the Viking invasions.

Erected by the Museum of London and Wates City of London Properties and unveiled by The Rt. Hon., The Lord Mayor, Sir David Rowe-Ham, G.B.E., on 25th November, 1986.

Pieces of hair hanging down in front of the lens

Camera lens covers on strings hanging loose
Cob webs

Fingers in the way

Particles such as dust and water droplets can be lit up by the flash. These particles need to be within a few centimeters of the camera lens, meaning very close in both proximity and plane as the camera lens axis. Since the air we breath is not particle free, it seems the chance of this occurring is very high. Most buildings are inhabited by microscopic flying insects that we can't see with our eyes but can be seen by the camera. They survive all year round, especially with central heating and air. Have you ever seen those little light balls on night vision video that seem to move rapidly and sporadically? In the experiments that I have conducted, I have found water droplets to be more reflective than dust particles.

A question that arises is why haven't orbs been noticed before in previous decades. There probably have been anomalous images of this sort in pictures before, but they were few and far between and considered to be merely occasional film flaws.

How an Orb is Created

A dust orb is created because a solid, reflective, rough-textured airborne particle, such as a dust particle, is situated near the camera lens and outside the depth of field. In other words, out of focus. Some common characteristics of dust orbs in photographs may be showing some sort of nucleus due to the rough texture of the surface.

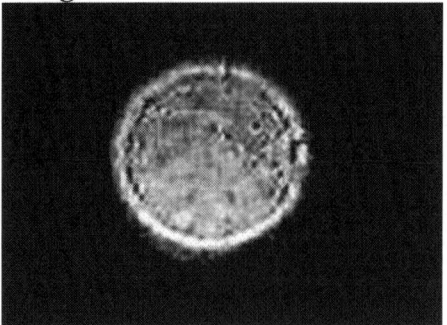

Dust particle blown up.

Orbs of a rectangular or octagonal shape are caused because an object with a shape similar to the aperture (the aperture is the hole that opens to let light through the lens) of the camera lens is out-of-focus (beyond depth of field range). The object will begin to take the shape of the aperture.

In other words, if the aperture of the camera is a hexagon, an out-of-focus dust orb will begin to take the shape of a hexagon, particularly towards the center of the image.

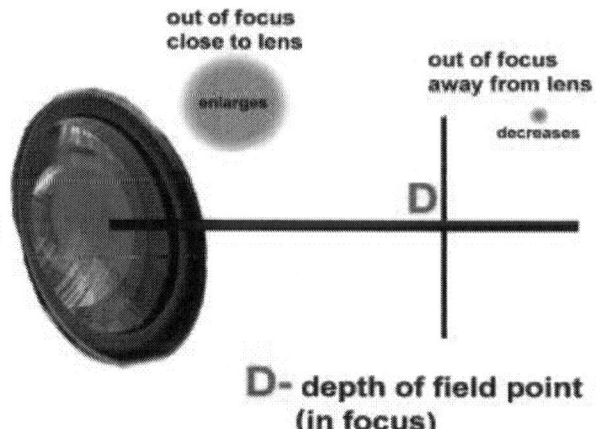

Naturalistic/Man-Made Ways

The newer photographic equipment is somewhat different from that available in previous decades in at least two ways. The first is the greater distance over which flash pictures can be taken, a result of increased film sensitivity ("speed" ASA 400 or 800 film) or in the case of a digital camera or a video camera, they use a "focal plane detector array," aka CCD (a charge coupled device plays the role of film in digitals), and an increased brightness of the flash itself. The overall increase in sensitivity and flash brightness results in a reach of up to 30 feet from the camera, whereas in the past one was lucky to get a good flash picture at 8 feet.

The second is the proximity of the flash unit to the lens, especially on the smaller cameras, being only 2-3 inches away, whereas in decades past the flash units were typically 5 or more inches away from the lens. The decreased distance between the flash and the lens means that the edge of the "beam" from the flash passes very close to the lens, decreasing the angle of reflection back into the lens.

Angle of Reflection

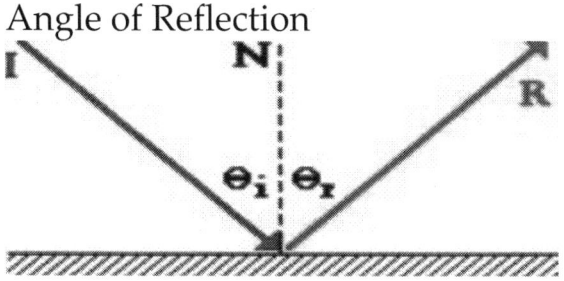

In the diagram above, the ray of light approaching the mirror is known as the incident ray (labeled I in the diagram). The ray of light, which leaves the mirror, is known as the reflected ray (labeled R in the diagram). At the point of incidence where the ray strikes the mirror, a line can be drawn perpendicular to the surface of the mirror; this line is known as a normal line (labeled N in the diagram). The normal line divides the angle between the incident ray and the reflected ray into two equal angles. The angle between the incident ray and the normal is known as the angle of incidence. The angle between the reflected ray and the normal is known as the angle of reflection.

Diffuse Reflection

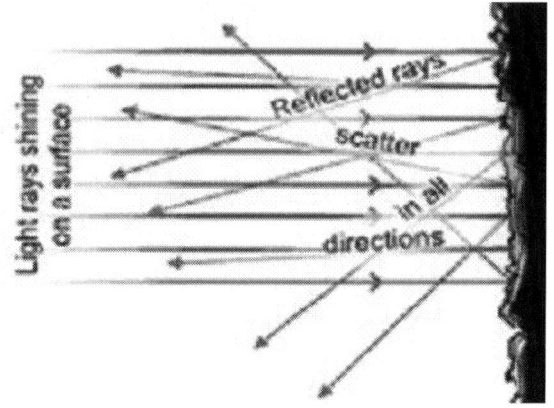

When light strikes a rough or granular surface, it bounces off in all directions due to the microscopic irregularities. Thus, an image is not formed. This is called diffuse reflection. The exact form of the reflection depends on the structure of the surface. Diffuse interreflection is a process whereby light reflected from an object strikes other objects in the surrounding area, illuminating them. Diffuse interreflection specifically describes light reflected from objects, which are not shiny or specular.

In real-life terms this means that light is reflected off non-shiny surfaces such as the ground, walls, or fabric, to reach areas not directly in view of a light source. If the diffuse surface is colored, the reflected light is also colored, resulting in similar coloration of surrounding objects.

Lens Flare

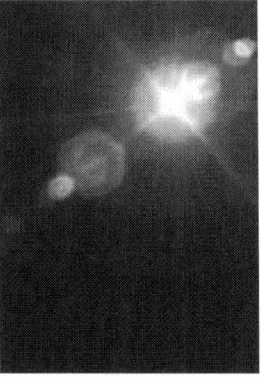

Lens flare from sun causing a hexagonal shape.

Another phenomena that is often mistaken for something paranormal is called "lens flare" which occurs when a bright light source (most often the sun) reflects off a portion of the lens and creates internal reflections of the aperture of the camera. Generally flare can be ruled out of most photos taken at night, but can be a problem with shooting pictures during the day.

Slow Shutter Speed

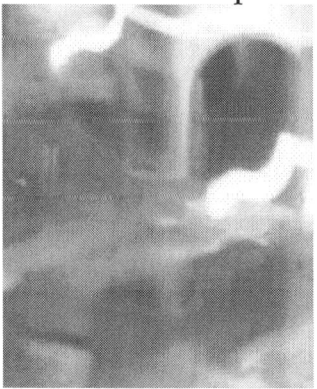

I cannot tell you how many photos I have seen from people who say, "Look, it's paranormal -- the ghost caused it to blur." No, the ghosts did not do it. It's called a slow shutter speed. The amount of light reaching the film or CCD is known as the exposure and this is controlled by two items on a camera -- the aperture and shutter speed.

The aperture is a variable hole in front of the lens that adjusts to let more or less light through, and the shutter speed is a cover over the film or CCD that controls the length of time that the light reaches the film. By adjusting the shutter speed you can control the movement of the subject. A fast shutter speed will freeze the subject and a slow shutter speed will make it look blurred as the subject moves. You can also combine flash with a slow speed to get movement and blur all in the same shot.

The aperture (how big or small the lens diaphragm inside a lens opens up) allows different amounts of light to fall onto film through the lens that's attached to your camera body. The shutter speed (the shutter curtain duration) controls how long it opens up to absorb the amount of light that falls onto film.

Light
Light is electromagnetic radiation with a wavelength that is visible to the eye (visible light).

The three basic dimensions of light are:

Intensity (or amplitude), which is related to the human perception of brightness of the light,
Frequency (or wavelength), perceived by humans as the color of the light, and
Polarization (or angle of vibration), which is not perceptible by humans under ordinary circumstances.

Light entering the eye is absorbed by light-sensitive pigments within the rod cells and cone cells in the retina, which creates electrochemical nerve pulses that travel through the optic nerve to the brain, producing what we call vision.

Color and Wavelength
Color results from an interaction between light, an object, and the viewer. All three elements must be present for color to exist as we know it. Light is reflected off the object and back into the viewers' eyes, this is how we see color. If you are holding a red rose and you turn away from that rose will it still be red?

The answer is no, all 3 conditions are no longer present.

Film cameras are based off of visible light. They can only record what's in the visible spectrum, not outside. They have faster film speeds but that only means the coatings on the film are made to be more sensitive to low light. Film has three layers which respond to green, blue, and red -- the same as the human eye. The human eye can only sense three colors, blue (B), green (G) and red (R), but through a balanced mixture of these three colors, we are able to see all colors. The camera cannot take a picture of something that's not visible, however it can see a different light angle than you.

If two people are standing side by side and one sees a ghost and the other does not, it doesn't mean it wasn't there. The other person could be at a different angle of reflection and not be able to see it.

The light we see with our eyes is really a very small portion of the electromagnetic spectrum. The region of the electromagnetic spectrum that is visible to a person's eye ranges from 400 to 700 nanometers. This is a mere slice of the massive electromagnetic spectrum. Wavelengths are measured in nanometers, which is one-billionth of a meter. Each wave is described by its wavelength -- the length from wave crest to adjacent wave crest. We use many of the invisible waves beyond the visible spectrum in other ways -- from short wavelength x-rays, to the broad wavelengths that are picked up by our radios and televisions.

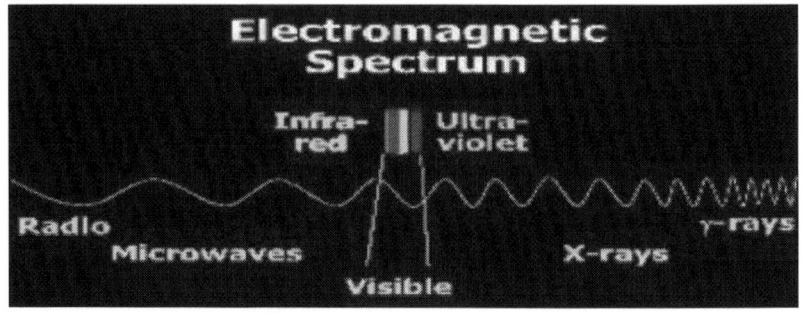

The Electromagnetic Spectrum

Our eyes have light sensors that are sensitive to the visible spectrum's wavelengths. When light waves strike these sensors, the sensors send signals to the brain. These signals are often perceived by the brain as a particular color. Exactly which color is seen depends on the composition of wavelengths in the light waves. For example, if the sensors detect all visible wavelengths at once, the brain perceives white light. If no wavelengths are detected, there is no light present and the brain perceives black.

Visible light is typically absorbed and emitted by electrons in molecules and atoms that move from one energy level to another.

The rainbow shows the visible part of the spectrum, infrared (if you could see it) would be located just beyond the red side with ultraviolet appearing just beyond the violet end.

The intervening frequencies are seen as orange, yellow, green, and blue.

Some animals, such as bees, can see UV radiation while others, such as snakes, can see infrared light.

However, because UV is a higher frequency radiation than visible light, it very easily can cause materials to fluoresce visible light. Fluorescence is the process wherein a molecule absorbs a photon of radiant energy at a particular wavelength and then quickly re-emits the energy at a slightly longer wavelength. According to modern theory, electrons are arranged in energy levels as they circulate around the nucleus. When electrons gain or lose energy, they jump between energy levels as they are rotating around the nucleus. As electrons gain energy, they move to the third, or outer, level. As they lose energy, they move to the inner or first energy level. One of the ways a molecule can gain energy is by absorbing light. If a molecule absorbs light, the energy of the light must be equal to the energy required to put the molecule in one of the higher energy states. When a molecule reaches an excited state, it does not stay there for very long, but quickly returns to a lower energy state either by emitting light or by colliding with another atomic particle.

How Do Infrared Cameras Work?
Cameras that can detect infrared and convert it to light are called night-vision cameras or infrared cameras. These are different from image intensifier cameras, which only amplify available visible light.

Infrared and thermal energy is light that is not visible because its wavelength is too long to be detected by the human eye. It is the part of the electromagnetic spectrum that we perceive as heat. Infrared allows us to see what our eyes cannot. Thermal radiation will not be recorded by infrared film because infrared films are not sensitive to a long enough wavelength to show such things as heat patterns.

Thermal infrared imagers are detector and lens combinations that give a visual representation of infrared energy emitted by objects. Thermal infrared images let you see heat and how it is distributed. A thermal infrared camera detects infrared energy and converts it into an electronic signal, which is then processed to produce a thermal image and perform temperature calculations. Thermal imaging cameras have lenses, just like visible light cameras. But in this case the lens focuses waves from infrared energy onto an infrared sensor array. Thousands of sensors on the array convert the infrared energy into electrical signals, which are then converted into a false-color image.

Infrared can be used as a way to measure the heat radiated by an object. This is the radiation produced by the motion of atoms and molecules in an object. The higher the temperature, the more the atoms and molecules move and the more infrared they produce. Any object that has a temperature above absolute zero (-459.67 degrees Fahrenheit); radiates in the infrared. Absolute zero is the temperature at which all atomic and molecular motion ceases.

Even objects that we think of as being very cold, such as an ice cube, emit infrared. When an object is not quite hot enough to radiate visible light, it will emit most of its energy in the infrared. For example, hot charcoal may not give off light but it does emit infrared, which we feel as heat. The warmer the object, the more infrared it emits. We experience infrared radiation every day. The heat that we feel from sunlight, a fire, a radiator, or a warm sidewalk is infrared. Although our eyes cannot see it, the nerves in our skin can feel it as heat. The temperature-sensitive nerve endings in your skin can detect the difference between your inside body temperature and your outside skin temperature.

Infrared light may be invisible to the naked eye but most digital cameras have CCD chips that are sensitive to both the visible spectrum and the near-infrared spectrum. I've heard some digital cameras may possibly see into the UV spectrum also, I don't know that part for a fact though just hearsay at this point; I haven't tried any experiments on that end.

Video cameras with night vision capabilities seem to show orbs in motion, well bad news guys this is merely the infrared camera picking up the IR LED patterns. The LED (Light Emitting Diode) throws off a beam of light invisible to the human eye, but seen by the night vision cameras. The cause is two infrared LEDs mounted just beneath the lens on every model. These act exactly like mini headlights, sending an IR beam out to about 6ft in front of the camcorder. Sorry, no ghost here.

Digital Cameras

The way the CCD sees the world is very different from the way we see it or a film camera sees it. We already know about the IR sensitivity of the CCD. All CCDs rely on software to construct the image from the millions of individual pixels. In consumer cameras this software needs to "compress" the raw data in order to get enough pictures onto the storage media or memory. This compression and the software compression algorithms vary, not only from different makers but even across the maker's own range of products.

A 3 megapixel CCD actually captures less than ¼ of the total image information available within a scene when compared with a 35mm camera negative. The software has to fill in the gaps in the image by making mathematical calculations with the information from neighboring pixels, thus a single pinpoint of light in a scene may be ignored completely or seen and then "expanded" by the software as it compares and interpolates each pixel. This can cause a mix of out of place pixels to fall into places causing some people to claim to see faces and images in digital pictures because of shaded pixels.

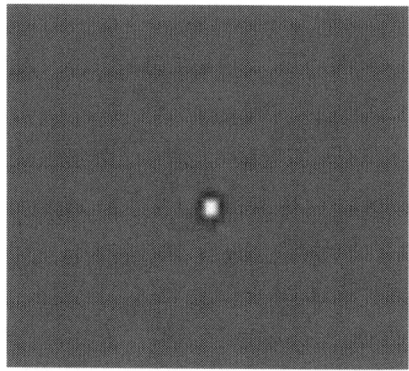

This is a missing pixel. It's square.

Testing your camera
Use the "TV remote test" to determine if your digital camera is sensitive to infrared light. Television remote controls use infrared light to turn the TV on and off and to change channels. Aim your TV remote control at the lens of your digital camera from a few inches away, push a button on your remote, and view the image on the LCD panel (not the optical viewfinder) of the camera. If you see a white flash of light coming from the TV remote on your camera's LCD screen, you've just determined that your camera is infrared-sensitive.

IR beam off on remote control

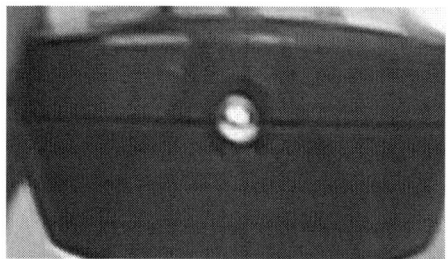

IR beam on if camera is sensitive

Non-Naturalistic

"Spirit Orbs" are sometimes said to exist more densely around certain haunted regions or to be the spirits of departed loved ones. These types of orbs are sometimes said to have faces, often with discernable expressions and even of recognizable persons. Some feel the size of an orb indicates how great of an impact a life force had in its life time.

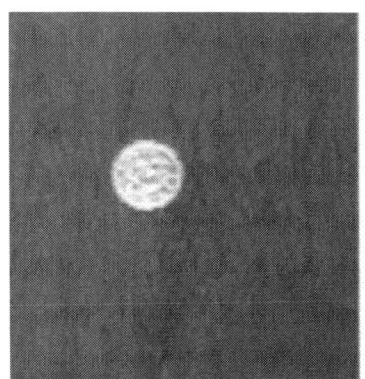 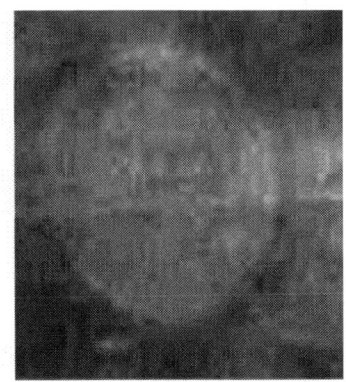

This is a picture of a dust orb... nothing more. Another view of spirit orbs holds that they are non-human spirits, with blue and red orbs symbolizing angels and the devil respectively. Another interpretation of colors in orbs is sex differentiation -- blue for male spirits, and red or pink for female, or that they indicate what mood the spirit is in. If orbs are energy they should be emitting light. Spirit orbs are also felt by some to be curious friendly protectors, particularly of children.

The paranormal belief in orbs is not so straightforward as those who believe that they are simply photographic artifacts.

An often encountered saying is, "Orbs are considered by some people to be the simplest and most common form of a disembodied spirit," but this concept is not supported by all within the paranormal field.

There are those who maintain that the orbs are caused by:

Ghosts/spirits
Angels/guardian spirits
Aliens
"The Little People" -- elves, pixies, fairies
Interdimensional beings

Even those "true believers" who steadfastly maintain that orbs are of paranormal origin are often forced to concede that dust may be the cause of most orb photos. A subset of these believers say that they can tell the difference between "dust orbs" and "real" (spirit) orbs, sometimes from a close examination of the image, or because of how they felt or were acting at the moment the photo was taken. Some true believers say that the orbs respond to spoken requests to appear, move, or appear as different colors.

Possible Real Orbs

Strange light in Triangular Field in Gettysburg (No, it's not a lightning bug.)

Supposedly haunted house.

Whatever your belief is when it comes to orb photos, things may not always be what they seem. Just keep in mind to look carefully at what you see and look around you, be more aware of your surroundings when taking a photo. Look for reflective things, don't just point and shoot, as I have seen many people do. I hope some of this information is helpful when trying to decide for yourself what is in your pictures.

Thank you to Rosemary Ellen Guiley, Jamie Henkin, and Lynda Lee Macken

Thanks to

http://www.ghostvillage.com

Parascience:
http://www.parascience.org.uk/misc/method/orbs.htm

Wikipedia:
http://en.wikipedia.org/wiki/Orb_(paranormal)

The Physics Classroom:
http://www.glenbrook.k12.il.us/gbssci/phys/Class/refln/u13l1c.html

Dr. Bruce Maccabee: http://brumac.8k.com/orb2.html
NDT Resource Center

Kodak: http://www.kodak.com

Made in the USA
Monee, IL
17 April 2022